Copyright © 2017 by Chrissy Stockton.

This book was designed by KJ Parish and published by Thought Catalog Books, a publishing house owned by The Thought & Expression Company. It was printed in the United States and was published in an edition of 1,000 copies.

ISBN 978-1-945796-43-2

WE ARE ALL JUST
A COLLECTION OF CORDS

CHRISSY STOCKTON

INDIAN SUMMER

This fall has been a series
of false starts.

I pack my window AC unit away
just to drag it out in the middle of the sticky night
when I can't stand the heat.

I take your name out of my phone
and add it in again
when I decide I don't want to give up on us
after all.

I breathe a sigh of relief
every time I fix a problem and say,
"wow, I am glad that is finished."
As if problems are solved once and then leave you
forever.
As if they don't continue to come around.

Maybe it's a sign that this summer heat won't go away.
Maybe it is stubborn just like my need to pack up
too soon.

I wish the Farmer's Almanac would tell me what
this means.

I wish the Farmer's Almanac would tell me when and how and why.

All I know is that this is our Indian summer
we keep going on and on
and I am ready for it to just be fall.

SOMEONE NEW

You came over in the late afternoon and did things like
pull my body into yours
by using your teeth as a lasso around my lower lip.

By night my pillows still smelled like you. How did
you make soap smell so good?

All night I was rolling over and smelling you.
All night I was rolling over and thinking about how
you make me forget
which way all my limbs are supposed to go.

You send me a picture on Snapchat
when you can't sleep
and I think I am supposed to think something about
the way you look
but all I can see is that mouth.

And all I can think is how
I want to bury my face in the painful Velcro
of your neck
and rub my lips raw.

POLITICALLY INCORRECT

I know I'm not supposed to say this
but the smell of tobacco on you
does things to me
I would not want my mom—
or the Surgeon General—
to know.

SEEING YOU AT YOUR PARTY WITH ANOTHER WOMAN

I bought four identical bottles of champagne
and gave one to you
to warm your house.

To the party I brought
three poems about fruit—
one borderline pornographic—
because I couldn't stop thinking about
what your face would look like when I read it to you.

But things didn't work out
as they often don't.

Instead of reading about lovers in bed.
Instead of seeing whether your lips would move in
response to my words.
I talked to your aunt about her new lake house
and enjoyed it.
And saw you across the room
with your girl
and didn't feel sad at all.

Love, I am learning, is too big
to just be about what I get out of it.

SPACE IS DUMB

I am not asking for much. I just want an entire galaxy to be created so that it can exist between us.

DEDICATION

I want you to know that you deserve no credit whatsoever for this poem.

You were not a muse. You were not inspiration.

You were a blank canvas I painted my love upon until it was beautiful.

I could buy more of you
for $7.99 at the art supply store,
or just order a stack from Prime.

Let me be clear: Everything that was good about us was good because I made it good.

I became a magician and waved my wand and pulled you from nothingness out of my hat.

When you see a magic show, who could be so mistaken as to think the rabbit is the brains of that operation? What did he do besides allow himself to be magicked into existence?

All along it was me who knew how to love so much.

It was me who knew how to make something beautiful ex nihilo,
me who saw your ordinariness and formed a picture of what it could become.

SIZE QUEEN

I'm sorry.
You leave me so unsatisfied.
I need to find someone with a bigger
heart.

SUNDAY RITUAL

Tonight I scrubbed all the corners of my apartment and then I stood under the hot shower and washed away all the bleach smell. I turned the lights off and lit candles and listened to the same Elliott Smith song on repeat. Then I laid on the couch and I thought about reading in bed and smoking and sending you text messages that say things like, "You know Hume was full of shit, right?"

WHEN I REALIZED I PROBABLY LOVED YOU

I related viscerally to a dish of ice cream
in the ecstasy of a summer afternoon.

Without warning it finds itself in a wet pool, not
remembering how or why.

Once you could have broken a spoon trying to get
me out.

Now I am so soft that I am begging
to be scooped up.

HOW TO GET RID OF A GHOST WHO HAS ALREADY GOTTEN RID OF YOU

I invited him over when he had already become a ghost because I wanted to see him in the light of day. I put my lips on him and smelled him and pressed my fingertips against his body.

He was solid. In the afternoon light he was just a man; he didn't have the power to haunt me the way I thought he did.

I could see now that there was nothing here to miss.

I could trace the edges of the mistake I had made, that same familiar shape. I had done the thing that girls with open minds and functioning hearts do. I had contemplated forever with this extraordinarily ordinary collection of molecules.

If you ask a ghost hunter, they will tell you there are distinct types of hauntings.

Demonic hauntings are said to be the product of an evil spirit attempting to take over an individual's body (possession). Poltergeists are noisy and mischievous pockets of energy that move things around aimlessly. Intellectual hauntings are less troublesome: a hearty "go toward the light" and some sage can clear your problem right up.

A residual haunting is the saddest of all. There's no ghost in the way we think of them, no brains of the operation. There's just some assemblage of energy that's fastened in time, repeating the same thing over and over. Whatever event happened had enough energy that there's a trace left in that place, a loop that never leaves.

It's a memory, physicalized in the most depressing way possible.

It's the same when you love someone deeply. That love gets stuck inside you. It repeats itself and you get confused thinking you want something that is no longer an option. You don't, really—it's just muscle memory. A longing that is no different than catching the scent of someone's perfume in the air long after they have left the room. You did something for so long that you have to practice not doing it in the awkward way you have to practice breathing in and out at a normal pace when you're trying to calm yourself down.

The thing about a residual haunting is you can't actively work at getting rid of it; you just stop noticing it after a while. This is a play that is going to go on with or without your attention. It is made up of human things and science things and other stuff we haven't worked out yet—but it's not for you.

A memory might not leave you alone the way you want it to, but it can't hurt you. It's mortal the way we are; it dies when you neglect it.

THE KNOWLEDGE OF GOOD AND EVIL

I want to solve the mystery that is you, but every time I think of a question I want to ask I also think, "That's something only a psycho would do," and I am trying to be detached.

I am paranoid of men's paranoia about how easily women fall for them or "act crazy" or whatever other ways we separate ourselves from each other in order to feel good.

In my ideal world I pull into a visitor's center with maps and pamphlets about who you are and what you see in me and what you don't.

Because I think that all this knowledge will help. That I can walk into it like a fortress and feel secure.

I am trying to remember that we still don't really understand why flowers bloom. I feel better when I remember that we have not yet even discovered all the things that are undiscoverable, but we make our way through life anyway. Knowledge doesn't solve our problems the way our thirst for it claims it will.

But then I remember the way Eve was tempted and how upset it made me as a child reading Bible stories.

How could a tree be bad? How could knowledge?

There's something wrong with a god or a man who could explain everything but asks you to take it on faith alone.

IRL DEATHBED

The problem with being from a Nordic family is that
no one ever expresses any emotion.

So when something happens
and all the men in your family sob for the first time
it feels like every molecule in your body is breaking.
Or bursting.
Or trying to escape the confines of your skin.

The problem is they will try to be strong for you.
When you just want them to be okay
with feeling weak.

One of the last things my grandfather said
to my grandmother,
his wife of 58 years,
as he sat bewildered
at the side of her deathbed,
is that she had a Band-Aid on her finger and he
couldn't recall why.
And never would.

When the actual dying started,
the room cleared out a bit.
Some of us stayed to keep her company.
Some of us took to the hall

out of some sense of decency.
Each felt a sense of pride in their decision.
Mine as a person who broke easily,
but never completely.

When my grandmother laid dying
the chaplain prayed a prayer that I,
born and raised in the church,
had never heard
or paid attention to.

May death come as easily as nightfall.

Later, when I turned from her body gasping for breath
the sun had set.
Night had come easily. And without me noticing it.

THE MIRACLE OF A VERY GOOD ENDING

There is a thrill in walking to and from places in the fall.

There is the confetti of leaves
and our last frivolous act of the season is
to step on them
just to hear them crunch.

There is the thrill of the darkness that comes early
of the relief of going home and going to bed
after a long, hot summer.

I have always loved fall because it is the season where
the things around us prepare to die.

I like to know that things end.

That there is a period at the end of a sentence.

That it doesn't matter if it is a good bit of prose or
something a student writes; we give them both the
courtesy of a standard-issue punctuation mark.
Of acknowledging that they are over.

I like to know that every year winter comes.

The summer days don't last.

That the trees will make a show of losing their leaves and then be quiet.

It is comforting to know we are not expected to muster up the courage to keep on going forever.

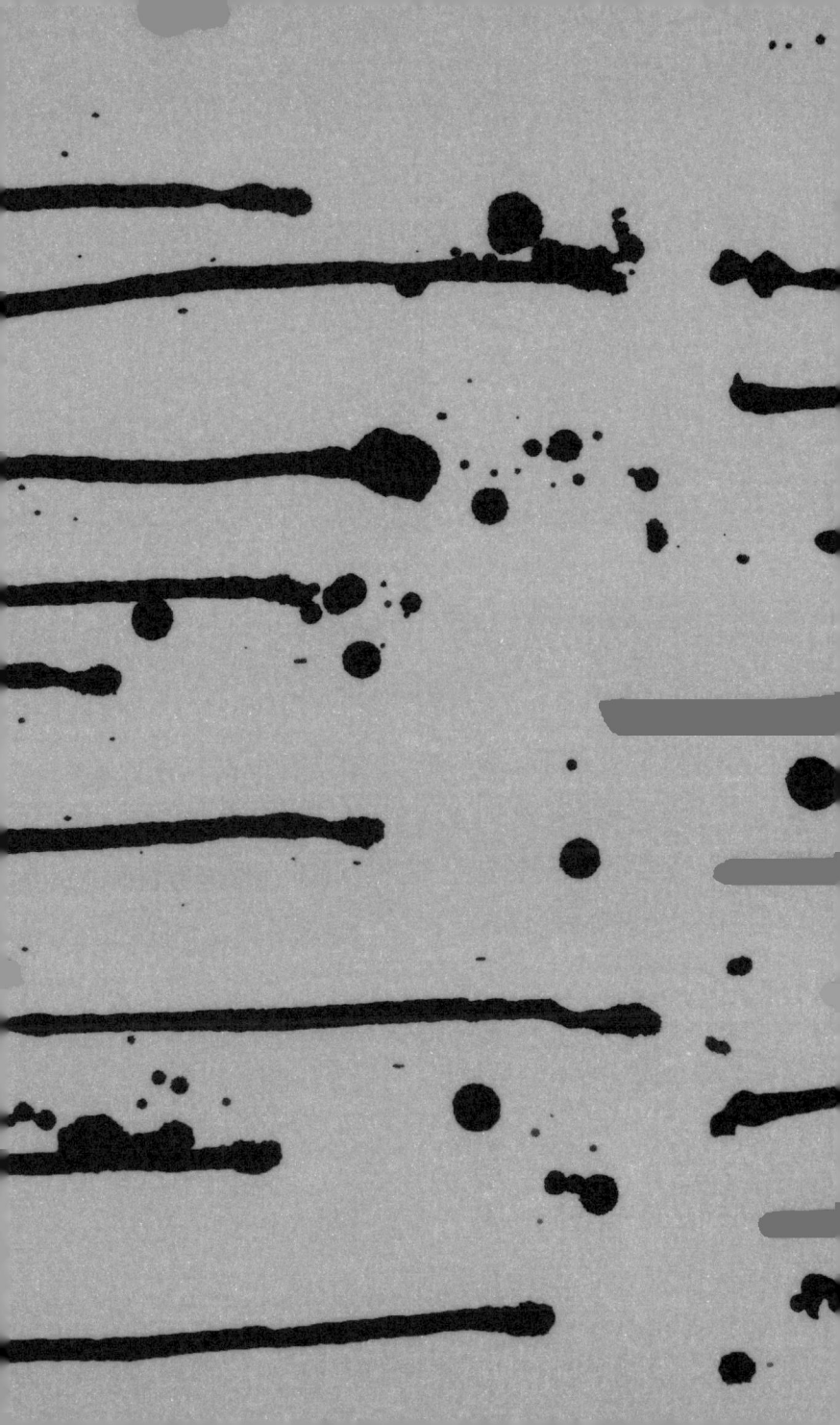

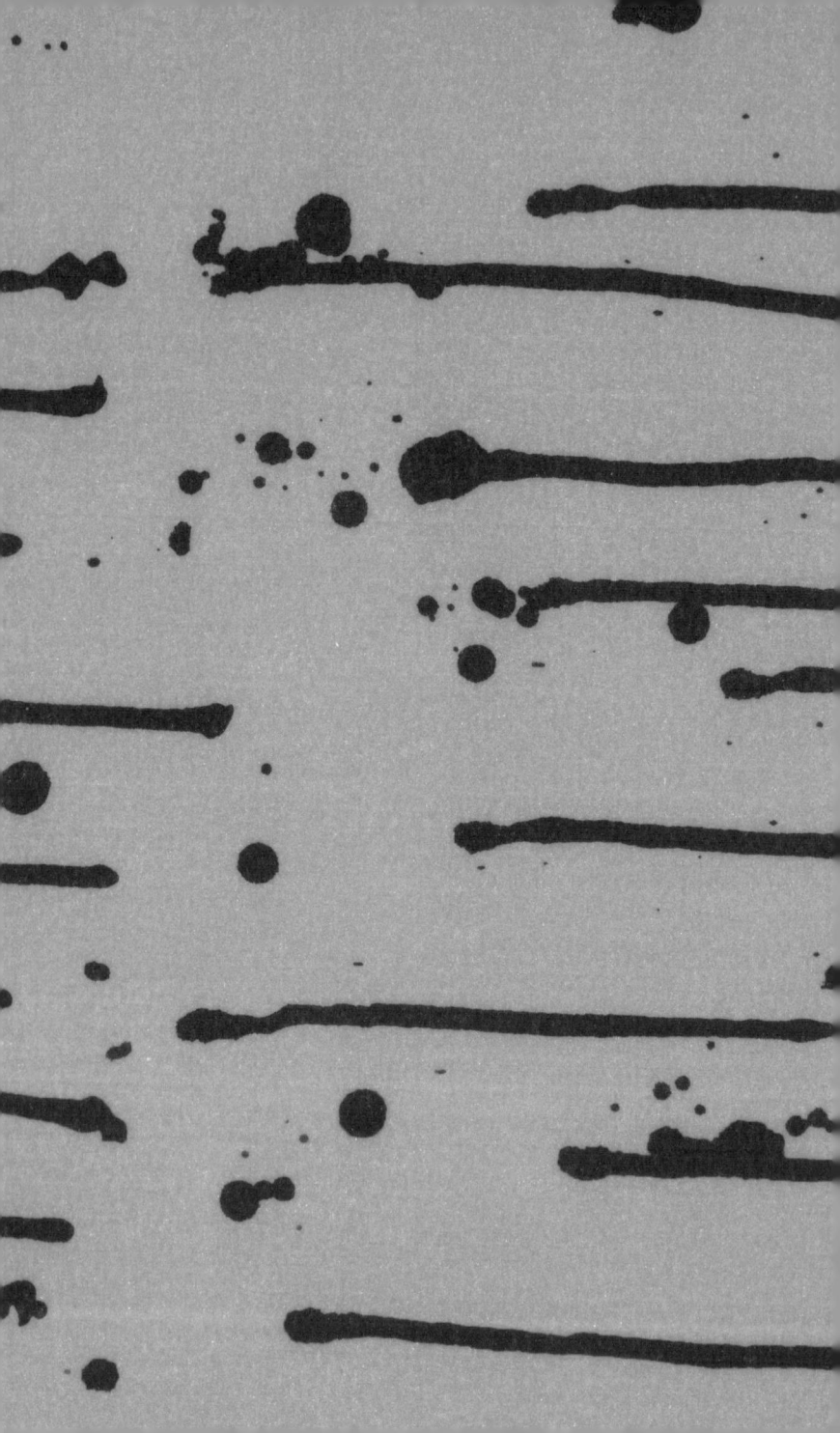

WHAT INSTAGRAM HAS TAUGHT ME

Freedom is just letting go of all the things I want everyone to notice about me.

EVERYONE ON TWITTER IS WRONG

It is not my job to be a justice dispenser.

It is not my job to be a justice dispenser.

It is not my job to be a justice dispenser.

It is not my job to be a justice dispenser.

It is not my job to be a justice dispenser.

It is not my job to be a justice dispenser.

It is not my job to be a justice dispenser.

It is not my job to be a justice dispenser.

It is not my job to be a justice dispenser.

It is not my job to be a justice dispenser.

I WONDER IF I WILL REMEMBER THIS AS THE WINTER WHEN EVERYONE DIED

My grandparents went like a Nicholas Sparks story.

My grandmother first: a surprise to us all.

My grandfather second: no surprise to anyone. He spent 58 years with his beloved; what promise could the earth hold now?

I include my dog next (guiltily, because you're not supposed to feel as bad for animals as you do for humans). Only two and a half and full of more love to give than I'd ever seen in a pup—never happy unless he was curled around your body.

I'd always wanted that and I couldn't decide if his disposition was an answer to prayer or if he just knew his life was going to be short (and he wanted to get it all out).

I wonder if I will remember this as the winter where everyone died but I wasn't overcome with sadness.

There has been a magic to this year, to 30. Suddenly I can be sad without it overpowering me. Suddenly sadness isn't my whole world. I can taste without being consumed. I can see more of the lay of the land.

I know there are places besides this; I know there are feelings besides this.

The last time someone died it was an uncle I barely knew. One of my stepfather's numerous brothers-in-law (Catholic) that I'd seen once a year for half my life but never noticed in the sea of people. I felt like a violation then; his daughter was my age and she stayed at my parents' house with her husband. I was intruding on their grief all week and also feeling lonely because they had each other and I never feel that way in a crisis. I always feel like I need to be okay just having myself, and I still don't know if that is the right way to feel.

The last time a dog died I panicked every time it became more apparent that his time was coming—for two straight years. When he fell down the stairs, when he stopped getting up from the floor when people knocked on the door, when he stopped making the big jump into bed to keep me company at night, I grieved all of these little deaths.

This time, I just grieved once. I don't know if that is an improvement or if the world is making me cold.

I wonder if I will remember the cold this winter even though it was warmer than usual. The agony of warming up my car in -17 degrees, or that it waited until

Christmas for the snow to stick.

I wonder why I am waiting around to see how I will feel in hindsight, as if that is The Marker that makes something real, the Hegelian eagle that will make a final decision about whether the winter was good or bad.

I drove up to the big lake yesterday because I wanted to see freshwater instead of all that ice, ice, ice. There was the snowy shore and the waves and the steam of heat from something somehow not frozen. Everything all together like the way it is with this death in the middle of a very good year.

Maybe that will be the memory: the thawed sea and the icy earth and me, the steam in between, trying to decide what form I am going to take.

IN RESPONSE TO ANOTHER ARGUMENT ABOUT BEING TOGETHER

I said: "You know, they don't even believe in the scientific method anymore?"

I'd read that somewhere, possibilities are infinite and testing is finite, so all the faith we put in science is just that—faith. At some point we all want to close up our books and go home. We pick a spot to say "enough" and call it a day.

We were in bed and I wrapped myself around him and felt his body loosen. I wasn't sure if he was waiting to see where my hands would end up or if he liked my argument.

I couldn't understand why he was so closed. Why he was convinced of our premature doom. Why he only saw the stars as fixed points and not the sky as a whole—full of negative space that made all the things that worked so much more beautifully in the way they mustered themselves into existence.

There was a poem I liked to read to him, because he was always so sad about failing. It reminded the reader to think about Icarus and his wax wings and that he only fell because he flew first.

I guess that was the difference between us.

I could imagine myself failing beautifully—with the dignity of someone who has done the one and only thing we are called to do in this life: try.

But he was a realist, not a dreamer. He could only see the crashing into the ocean, not the beauty that preceded it.

AURORA BOREALIS

The lights in the sky have always meant home. The North. Miles of flat road and high beams and no one else around. A gift from above not meant to be explained or counted on or captured—just experienced.

They shut you up and glue you to your driver's seat on the side of the road where you pull over to watch them move.

You can't go out and find them; you can just hope that when the conditions are right they will come. You can only be ready to stop what you are doing if they choose to appear. You can only consent to their capricious ways.

It was like that with us; I couldn't make you do anything. I couldn't make you love me or believe that I loved you. I could just be ready to stop those few times when things were good. Stop what I am doing and be in the moment, knowing it will not last.

I still read your emails sometimes when I want to be sad.

I still wonder if you were the one I was supposed to figure out how to be with, but I was too young and too dumb to figure out how to make you want to be with me.

You are still a fixed point in my history, even though I think I have also moved on.

Because I could set a watch by the times I think about you. You have become a benchmark in my life. The familiar thing I hope to catch in my rearview mirror when I am driving at night.

You are still a mark in the distance I can use to find my way. When your ghost comes around he is still comforting, familiar, fleeting.

When your memory finds me, you still feel like home.

DON'T @ ME

There could be a place for us. We could make a place for us.

2:45 AM

It is 2:45 in the morning and I think you are probably sending some other girl a text that says, "I can't sleep."

I know that this is the purpose women serve in your life. They are sheep you can use to count your way to sleep.

I am counting, too. I wonder how many nights it will be until I stop wanting to be one of them.

ANOTHER STORM, 3:30 AM

It's storming out again
and you are in bed texting me that the only thing that
would make this storm better
is my mouth.

The thunder is loud and my fear makes it hard to
breathe.

There's a lot that I'm afraid of these days,
a lot of reasons I don't like to lie in bed awake.
It's the fear thoughts and the fear of the fear thoughts.

It's having to keep my fingers off the right buttons
so that I won't go texting you.

I'm driving to Colorado soon and
I wish I would wonder whether I'll think about you
instead of knowing I will,
instead of looking in my rearview mirror the whole
damn time.

There will be mountains in front of me
(mountains!),
and I will be looking in the rearview mirror.

I see flashing lights in the sky.
At first I can't believe there are planes up there
and then I remember
I know what it's like to want to get away from something so badly.

YOU WON'T READ THIS

I'm not falling apart anymore. I thought you should know that.

There's an uncertainty that I used to wear as a badge of honor. I'm better than that now.

I'm better now.

If I'd been like this when you came around, maybe things would be different.

But I didn't change for you.

I just changed.

ACTUAL RELATIONSHIPS

I understand that you don't know what to say when you ask how my day was and I say things like, "I wrote three poems today."

The way I don't understand how you are always eating those sour pomegranate seeds.

Or why you think my love is less worthwhile because I'd stoop so low as to give it to you.

WATCHING SOMEONE REALIZE THERE ARE PLANETS BESIDES THIS

In a fifteen-passenger van, my friends and I are on the way to camp at the coast and someone near the back exclaimed, "I've never seen the ocean before!" And I turned to see there were glimpses of blue and white waves crashing in a gap between buildings as we drove past at 75 MPH.

THE NIGHTLY NEWS

Tonight: the way you make me feel.

A developing story: your mouth.

Investigation: your skin smells like home.

Human-interest story: Please don't leave me.

Breaking news: I am awake. I am alive. You are a fire and there is something inside me that wants to burn.

A DAY'S WORK

Did you write a poem today? Did you feel happiness today?

Did you stop in the middle of an ordinary task to wonder at the size of the universe and the magnitude of your heart and feel satisfied?

Did you love? Did you feel loved?

Were you moved? Did you move someone?

Did you create?

Did you participate wholly in your strange and wild life?

Were you soft? Did you try to be fearless?

Did you worry and rise out of the worry?

How did you become more aware of your powerful presence in this world than you were yesterday? How did you respond to your own beating heart? The one that keeps beating.

What did you do to honor how brave it is that you go on and on?

SOMEONE NEW II

The moment when
another man's lips
touch yours

and the world opens up

and you feel so sorry
for ever believing
the world was small enough
that he could have made you feel full.

SOMEONE NEW III

Being with him was a fact-finding mission.

Like I was sent to discover all the things about you
that weren't so special
after all.

In the stark contrast of someone else's affection, I could see how flimsy yours was. How it dissolved when I poked at it, how it should have been too weak to pass inspection.

There is a reason why lives are long. We need so desperately to make so many mistakes, it is hard to fit them all in.

SATURDAY NIGHT WRITING POEMS

You are out drinking and I am lying on my floor writing poems. I am not sure if this is romantic or just sad.

This is the scene of a John Mayer song, but there is an aspirational quality to a pop star's loneliness that I'm not sure I merit. I'm 31 and I don't know if it's cute anymore to be lonely.

I think I have crossed an invisible line.

I am not a heartsick teen.
My biopic will not be posthumously directed by John Hughes
or Nora Ephron.

I'm not sure I'm the one you root for anymore, or if I am too far gone.

SOLID BODIES

When I can't sleep, I Google your name just to make sure you are still there.

Nothing seems real in these in-between hours and sometimes I wonder if I made it all up.

I can find you on my phone and look at your face and remember how solid your body felt next to mine.

There are emails I can read from this other world, flirtations and arguments about god and the feeling that everything would last.

I like to know that I'm not crazy. I like to browse the evidence that you are a real even if now you are in another city interacting with someone else's solid body.

SUMMER ANGELS

I walked behind you in the pitch dark, and the smell of tobacco surrounded you like a halo. Not to be cheesy, but I always thought of you as an angel anyway. The halo fit. You did me an angelic service. You woke me up to myself again.

That summer night we sat barefoot on your porch and drank out of tall glasses. I tried to let it not mean a lot to me because I think those things are always meaning a lot to me and other people don't really notice anything.

Later I asked you if what we saw from your bed was a street light; it couldn't be bright out already, but it was. I was worried about the metaphor of the way the sun was always coming up on us.

We closed the blinds and slept in.

UPTOWN IN LATE SPRING

I always think I will love summer the way people go on and on about fall.

But I get nervous about that much happiness.

The lawns in my neighborhood are combusting with people and parties and music, and I get worried that I am not living enough, that I am not keeping up.

I stay awake at night worrying about things like if the summer will pass and I will never be wearing Daisy Dukes and holding a red Solo cup in an Instagram photo.

I want to be in the sun; I just don't know if it's okay to be there all alone.

CITY MOUSE

After an extended stay in the mountains
I went to San Francisco and took a bus to Market
Street so I could sit in a cafe surrounded by the
people in the Financial District
and breathe.

My rural friends don't understand the thrill of the city. The way riding the bus can make you feel powerful because you aren't attached to it like a car. You can go anywhere if you want to and not worry. You don't have to always be going home.

SOMETHING ABOUT YOU AND YOUR MOUTH AND FRUIT

I want to bite into an apple and know that in the next moment your mouth will be full of it because you are hungry for your mouth to be all the places my mouth has been.

And I am hungry to watch you and your mouth and fruit.

You and I and that apple—
we both know we are going to eat it to the core.

A SERIES OF SENSATIONS

To you I am a series of sensations:
a wet mouth and a soft body and kind hands.
I am hair you fall asleep smelling.

To you I am impermanent, a temporary pleasure you
can fathom saying goodbye to.

You are a wolf and I am a lamb,
and the remarkable thing is
I keep coming back for more.

I CAN'T WAIT FOR THE DAY WHEN I AM BORED OF YOU

I wrote a list of things I like about you and it said things like "the smell of his skin relaxes me" and "perfect dick" and "the best kisser in the entire world, probably."

Below it I wrote a list of things I don't like about you. It was shorter and it ended with "he doesn't love me."

I don't know how to act around someone who won't tell me what he needs. I don't know if I should tell you how smart you are or if that's something you already know. I don't know if you have insecurities about women I need to assuage. I don't know if I need to tell you that your dick is perfect. That normally I don't have so much trouble forming sentences while someone is inside me.

I'm always worried about how people feel and whether they have been loved enough. I think when you are a person with anxiety, your mind can get away from you sometimes and you can think some pretty nasty thoughts about yourself. It gives you a lot of empathy. I don't like the idea of anyone else having to deal with those kinds of thoughts, so I try to give them ammunition in the form of reality. I tell them truthfully the things they don't have to worry about.

I don't think you think about any of these things, and it's the most exhausting part about being a woman. Before you, my head was full of things much more interesting and important than playing the same conversations on repeat and looking for clues that aren't there.

"I am dumber because of this relationship," I add to the second list.

I can't believe how capable I am of giving so much thought to someone who almost certainly is not thinking this much about me.

I can't believe how capable I am of being pathetic.

Whenever I get frustrated with something, I try to understand its purpose. As long as there's some kind of goal or reason for the pain, I can take it. It's self-administered logotherapy.

But I don't have enough experience to understand what the bigger picture is here. What am I learning? What do I get as my reward for cluttering my brain with these inane thoughts? Am I making it better for when I find someone else?

Maybe I will get bored soon. Maybe there are only so many minutes of your life that can be spent wondering what it means if he hasn't texted today and all those minutes are about to expire. Then I can just be happy and relaxed forever. Like you.

ANXIETY IN WINTER

Yesterday I walked to the store just to buy a bag of frozen peaches. I usually think fruit is too sweet, but I couldn't stop thinking about putting them in a cup with some soda water and sipping until they were warm enough to eat with my fingers.

There's a tip in the book I read over the summer about bringing your mail in and just reading it and responding to it immediately instead of setting it on the counter and walking away. Today I got some coupons and a bill and a check. I threw the coupons away and paid my bill and deposited my check on my phone and there was nothing left to think about and I could relax.

All I want to do lately is lie in the dark and listen to sad music and feel sad. I did this for four hours yesterday and two hours the day before. I light candles so I don't have to turn on the lights. I play the music from my phone so I don't have to get up to change it.

There is nothing left for me to do. There is nothing left for me to think about.

THE TITLE OF THIS POEM IS 'FUCKBOYS'

Losing you has been like
the incredible relief of an exhale
I have been waiting years
to take.

I didn't realize I had been struggling to swim to the surface for so long.

But here I am inhaling something new.

And spitting you out like salty water.

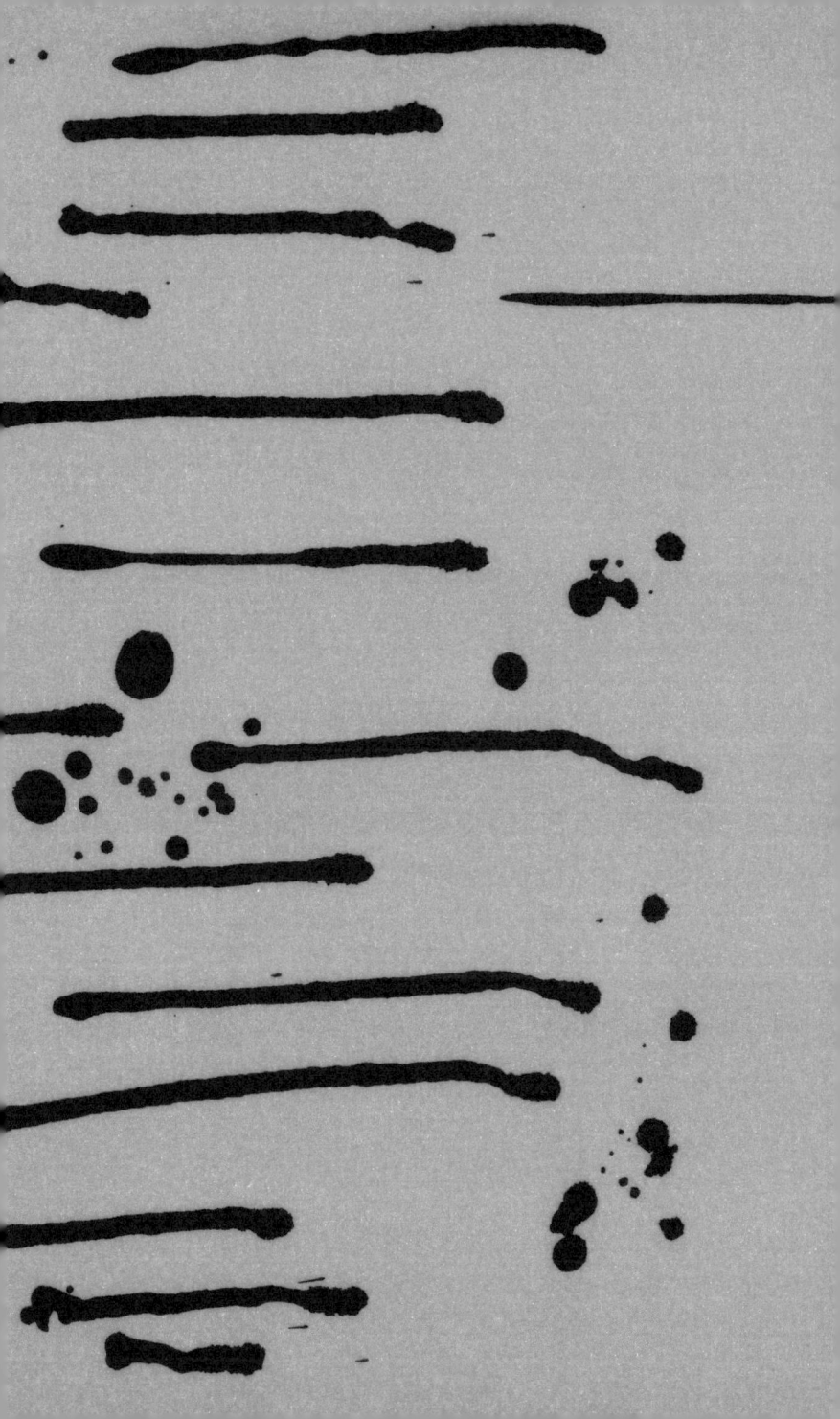

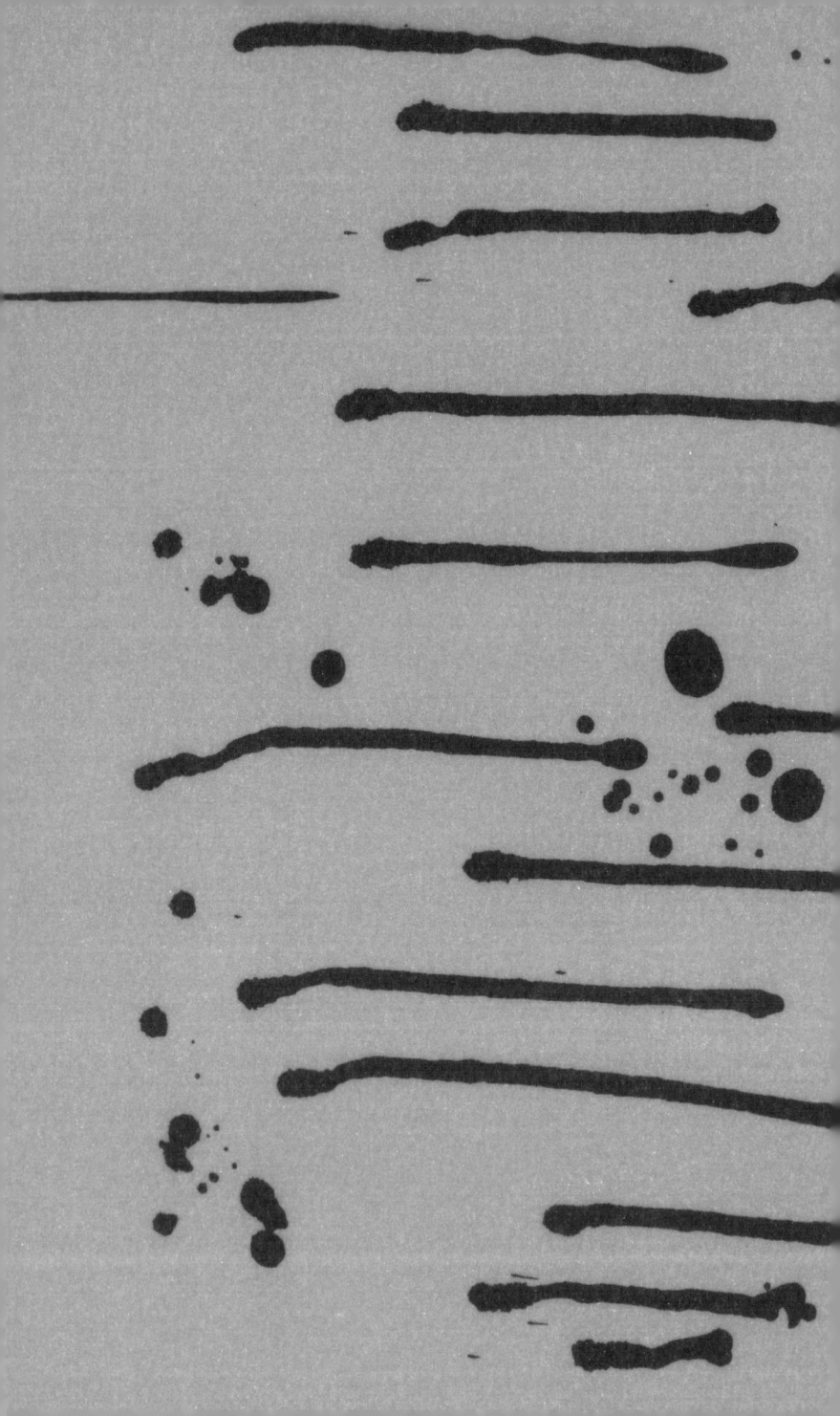

BREAKUP POEM

I just feel like

what can someone offer him
that is more
than what I have already offered?

And I don't want to hear the answer to that question.

COMING DOWN FROM THE HIGH OF BEING LOVED

I like two poems about happiness. One says you want to give up everything you have to be as happy as you were Back Then. The other says, "they didn't fill the desert with pyramids. They just built some."

I read them back-to-back hundreds of times the January I came home from the West Coast. I had left a mountain filled with people I loved very much to move home. I was terribly lonely and it was always dark outside and I was viscerally scared I wouldn't ever be as happy as I had been the previous few months.

I saw a picture on Facebook of a concert that was held in the cookhouse last week. Our cookhouse we once lit up with tea lights. Where we laid on the floor between the kitchen counters and talked about god. Where we played guitar and danced and when we ran out of steam we all sang hymns because they were the only songs we all knew by heart.

One night I threw a sleepover there for all the girls in Lincoln and Shayla, and I made trip after trip carrying heavy armfuls of wood from our woodhouse to the back door so we could stay warm. There was this thing about our friendship that meant we were always the ones carrying wood for people, because we knew there was a kind of joy in that. We had arms that worked and legs that carried us and were strong enough to not think about the possibility of a spider lurking somewhere in the pile when we stuck our hands into the dark.

I had to get over that place like a breakup. The second worst I've ever had.

It's hard to find a place where you are so happy and then move on. It's hard to push the upper limit of how full your heart can be and then go back and things just don't fill you up like they used to. Once I knew it was an option to love people so much and feel loved by them, I didn't know how to not exist in that place. I didn't know how to deal with the fact that we were all going to fall out of touch with each other.

Tom came to visit last summer and Paul and Shayla came in from the suburbs and we went to a bar downtown I go to all the time and it was funny to see how out of place these mountain men felt there. The next day I took Tom to my favorite dock and we laid on it and didn't talk about anything. I walked him to a concert where Paul was waiting and we hugged and said we wouldn't let so much time pass.

I don't think it's bad that we have moved on. Things don't go on forever. I am learning this even though I am also obsessed with the idea of fecundity.

It is just hard when something is good to not want more.

NO COMMERCIAL PURPOSE

Creation is the journey and the map and the road and the destination.

Creation is the billboard that tells you exactly where to exit.

It's Siri's instructional voice, it's the blood pressing against your keyboard with a thin sliver of skin holding it all in.

Creation is what comes out when your hands are moving faster than your brain is thinking—what occupies your mind when you are busy occupying your hands with something else.

Creation is the way the specific pen matters. Creation is the way a blank page stirs up an excitement in you that doesn't cease until it is covered in what you meant to cover it in.

Creation is the right music, the right amount of background noise, a full coffee in front of you and hours to make something happen. The joy of pressing on. The thrill of seeing on the page what you have not yet seen in your mind.

Creation is magic and the work ethic it takes to squeeze it all out.

Creation is a gift, but one that you have earned. A visitor you have gone to great lengths to cater to. A knock at the door you are expecting because you have spent all week preparing your house.

I HAVE SOMETHING WEIRD TO TELL YOU BEFORE I FORGET

I have to tell you something weird before I forget.

"Last month a 13-year-old boy abducted an eight-year-old girl. And when people asked him why, he said he learned about it on TV."

I love this poem about instructions for the first time you see a woman naked.

Because it will be on a screen.

And there are no instructions necessary when you are just watching.

Sometimes I wonder if I underestimate the clinical nature of the digital age. The way we swipe "yes" or "no" on people and move on.

But I don't think a generation can be any one thing. I love people, and I know others do, too, despite our birth years.

The world is cruel and already cruel enough. I want to find the space in each other to settle into.

I don't care if men tell me I am pathetic for loving them when you are supposed to just be cool. I think that is what human beings are made to do.

People have forgotten their lines. I have the script in front of me.

I DON'T WANT TO CHANGE YOU

I understand what it is to be human.

I can love you. I can leave you as you are.

WHAT I GREW UP DREAMING MY ADULT LIFE WOULD BE LIKE, WEIRDLY

I am sitting at a cafe that is playing French Montana too loud.

It's closing soon and I have to walk through the city in the dark after this.

I wrote three poems and am happy with them.

Walking home, more fragments will come.

WHEN SOMEONE MAKES YOU FEEL LIKE WHAT YOU HAVE TO OFFER ISN'T ENOUGH

You've already done the brave thing. You've already loved.

Even when you love the wrong person, even when you try to mold all the parts of them into something that might be good enough for forever—you are doing exactly what you are supposed to be doing. Trying and failing is a thing that comes before trying and succeeding.

Still, it hurts to be rejected. And it's important that you understand it hurts everyone. That girl you think you could be—the one who's perfect and always looks put-together—gets dumped, too. The most beautiful women in the world get rejected. The smartest, kindest, most likeable women in the world get rejected. Whatever shortcomings you think you have are not at fault for this.

If being deserving of love was about being perfect, the entire world would be single. It only takes a few minutes of delving into the romantic history of whatever women you admire to understand this.

There are less mysterious forces at play: People have conceptions about the kind of life they think they should have, and they want someone who fits that picture. They have baggage, they have preferences, they have fears—and these all affect the outcome of your relationship without ever taking into account how good or bad or deserving you are. Sometimes you really do screw up, but you'd already know if that happened, wouldn't you? Take solace in knowing the break is more about him than about you.

This is a hard time where you have to hold your head high. Allow yourself to hope for something better than the imperfect thing you need to let go of. Know that the difficult feelings won't last, even when they seem like they will. Everything is downhill from this moment when you understand that what happened is natural and normal and temporary.

No one tells a story that starts with the happy ending. This is what you need to do right now to get to where you want to be. Keep going.

LISTENING TO CLASSIC ROCK IN BIG SUR PAST MIDNIGHT

We are driving on the mountain road
late
listening to the radio
and we don't see any other cars.

Our hair is wet from the salty baths
we took in the springs on the cliff.

For hours the ocean crashed beneath us
we laid beside each other
supine and nude, listening.

And I swear I saw things in the stars
that were put there for me.

Just me.

We don't speak now;
there is nothing to say.

How can we talk about what has happened to us tonight?

It seems obscene to put it into words.

AFTER AN ELECTION, AFTER NINE DAYS OF WORRY, AFTER HIBERNATION

Laughing about how cheap
and how good
it was to buy three iced Americanos and drive around
the city
and drop one at Kyle's work.

Who knew that something would feel so good again?

WASTING HEAT IN A HOTEL ROOM ON THE NORTH SHORE

All day I keep walking over to the deck so that I can open up the doors and stick my head into the cold air and listen to the waves crashing onto rocks below.

For years I have been thinking about that song about dirt. I keep driving to beautiful places and Instagramming them just to say "makes you wanna build a ten percent down white picket fence house on this dirt."

There is something about these places that makes me finally feel like putting down roots. That makes me wish for a house and someone else in it. And dogs running around, always.

In my everyday life, I don't think I want to buy a house in the middle of nowhere. I don't want the guy for the sake of having the guy. I don't want to slow down or stop. I don't want to disappear.

But there's this mood I'm in when I'm someplace beautiful. I get reminded that I could have this life that is only made up of the things I want: earthy views and loving someone who understands how to be loved, animals and books and fires outside.

Even though it isn't that easy.

I was trying to explain to someone recently what I like about poetry. I said it's like how they feel about music. When it's good it takes you into the bigness of the moment. You get this clear picture of everything you care about.

It's the same feeling here in this place with those waves crashing, writing this poem. The things I want are naked and sturdy, ready to be born.

TOO MUCH WINE AND TOO MANY FRIENDS

There was another party. There were more people. More poems. There was another flash about the kind of person I want to be and the kind of life I want to live. There's a beach there somewhere and dogs and a big wooden table where we pour wine for all the people we know and laugh and eat and linger too long. I don't know who the people are. I don't know where the place is. I just know it smells a little bit like salt and I am always vacuuming because there is so much dog hair.

ABOUT THE AUTHOR

Chrissy Stockton is a writer, thinker, and creative cheerleader based on the internet. She has a degree in philosophy and if she could have any superpower she would be able to talk to dogs. *We Are All Just A Collection Of Cords* is her first poetry book. Follow her on Instagram @x.lane.s.

THOUGHT CATALOG Books

Thought Catalog Books is a publishing house owned by The Thought & Expression Company, an independent media group based in Brooklyn, NY. Founded in 2010, we are committed to facilitating thought and expression. We exist to help people become better communicators and listeners in order to engender a more exciting, attentive, and imaginative world.

Visit us on the web at *www.thoughtcatalogbooks.com*.

 Collective World

Thought Catalog Books is powered by Collective World, a community of creatives and writers from all over the globe. Join us at *www.collective.world* to connect with interesting people, find inspiration, and share your talent.

MORE POETRY FROM THOUGHT CATALOG BOOKS

Your Soul Is A River
—*Nikita Gill*

Seeds Planted In Concrete
—*Bianca Sparacino*

Bloodline
—*Ari Eastman*

All The Words I Should Have Said
—*Rania Naim*

THOUGHT CATALOG Books